NEW YORK CITY

Designed and Produced by

Ted Smart & David Gibbon

MAYFLOWER BOOKS · NEW YORK CITY

'New York, New York...
a city so nice they had to name it twice.'

JON Hendricks, who wrote a celebration of 'the beauty and the beast side' of New York City, wasn't the first, and surely won't be the last. The city must be the most celebrated in popular song of all; Paris or anywhere else must be way behind. The songs sing about the excitement, the romance, the rewards of making it in 'Baghdad on the Hudson'. One day in New York can also show you it can be the most depressing city in the world if you don't make it. Maybe the most glamorous manmade sight on earth is looking down Park Avenue to the Pan Am building at dusk when the myriad lights come on. And then the shocks, the sordidness are usually only a few steps away. New York is like that. A city where the latest is the greatest, dedicated to the idea of upward mobility. A trip to New York will make your heart beat faster – literally, they say, it's something to do with the electricity. It can also make you draw a deep breath of relief when you get back home again. Manhattan has got everything – the best and worst of city living. And it's only just over thirteen miles long, and two miles wide at its widest. Apart from the hardy souls who manage to live there (you know the old cliché, 'It's a great place to visit...*but*'), every working day four million people enter and leave Manhattan. Most New Yorkers don't live in Manhattan but in one of the other four boroughs that make up New York City, yet the island is still the kernel of the great big New York nut everyone comes to crack. One tenth of America lives in New York, and it's the capital in all but name and government.

First charted by Giovanni da Verrazano, sent by Francis I of France to open up the vast, unknown treasure chest of the New World, by the time of the American Civil War in 1861 New York led the continent in trade, manufacture, finance. Today, the city may be going broke. Blame, perhaps, the rich and semi-rich whose expenses and taxes kept the lifestyle going, who fled to greener pastures in the uneasy decade from 1950 to 1960, leaving the city to cope with its problems of protest and chronic poverty. So the highs and the lows are laid out in front of you – it's the sudden contrasts of the spectacular and the sordid that shock the visitor. But, and the statistics are stunning, New York leads America in money matters, communications and the industry that goes with it, buying and selling, fashion and clothing manufacture, and as a center for all the arts, not excluding the lively ones.

Five boroughs make up New York. Each one has its own character, and like Professor Higgins' London, its own accent. Staten Island, now linked to Brooklyn by the longest suspension bridge in the world, the Verrazano-Narrows, and to Manhattan by the famous ferry that made Cornelius Vanderbilt's fortune, is still green and countrified – you can make sassafras tea from the bark you peel off the big shady trees in your own back yard. Brooklyn, to the southeast of Manhattan, is the most industrialized, more heavily populated borough. It boasts New York's most popular beach, Coney Island and a black ghetto, Bedford-Stuyvesant, to rival Manhattan's Harlem with its hopes and horrors. Many famous people, like Mario Lanza, Barbra Streisand and the Dolly Sisters came from Brooklyn, which shows perhaps that it's a good place...to come from. Queens joins it to the East. It is the largest of the five boroughs, sandwiched between Brooklyn and elegant Long Island, where the rich live and the lucky go on weekends. Queens was named after Britain's King Charles II's wife and the most a casual visitor will see of it is the view on the way to Manhattan from one of the airports, La Guardia or Kennedy superport. Sports fans know Queens as the home of Shea Stadium, Aqueduct Racetrack, and Forest Hills, where the American tennis championships are held. The Bronx, the only borough on the mainland, is named after Johannes Bronck, the first European (he was a Dane) to settle north of the Harlem River. It is next to the top tip of Manhattan, has a famous Zoo and Botanic Garden, a historic sports place in Yankee Stadium, industry to the south and rich residents to the north, where it changes from Yonkers ('Where true love conquers,' as the song 'Manhattan' has it) into Westchester County.

But Manhattan is still the hub, the focus, the glittering prize of New York City – the 'Big Apple' as the jazz musicians of the 'thirties nicknamed it.

Look at a map of Manhattan through the years, and you will see that it grew from the bottom up. The French found it first, while looking for the fabled Northwest Passage to India. Then came Henry Hudson in 1609, who, working for the Dutch, established friendly relations with the local Indians. In the previous century five tribes in the area had succeeded in banding together in the legendary Great Peace, keeping down the internecine battling which was the constant factor in Indian life. Sometimes called the Five Nations, the Mohawks, Oneidas, Onondugas, Cayugas and Senacas formed a powerful Iroquois empire which maintained control to some extent over most of New York for a hundred and fifty years after the first white adventurers appeared. In the earliest known picture of New York, drawn in 1626 and captioned Fort Nieuw Amsterdam, you can see a windmill, a fort and a handful of houses in the Dutch style, with Indian canoes paddling across the foreground and tall ships tacking to and fro in the background. Greed was the spur; the quick, certain riches of fur trading appealed to the Europeans more than the hazards of farming. So friendly relations with the local Indians were a practical necessity. In 1624 the Dutch Government decided to make a permanent trading post on Manhattan Island. Thirty families came, tempted by promises of free passage and certain employment. In 1626 the first Governor, Peter Minuit, made the best real estate deal of all time. He bought the island from the local Manahasset Indians for twenty four dollars' worth of beads. Settlement prospered; in 1628 the first church was built. Then the peppery, peglegged Peter Stuyvesant became Director General, and New Amsterdam received a charter.

Stuyvesant built a protective wall where Wall Street is today, and a road to his farm – or 'bouwerie' – now the notorious Bowery. In 1833 his descendants gave the area, now known as Tomkins Square Park, to the City – his farm is now the East Village area famed as the 'New Bohemia' in the middle '60s. His bones lie in St Marks in the Bouwerie, one of the few buildings to survive from early times. His New York comprised about three hundred and fifty houses, with fifteen hundred people, speaking, though Dutch was the official language, about eighteen tongues. Cosmopolitan Manhattan had begun; by now the population included the first Jewish settlers, and blacks who came as slaves with the first settlers, together with English, Germans, French, Swedes and Scots. The Bronx, Queens, Staten Island and Brooklyn were, at that point, all thinly settled. Then in 1664 the territory was surrendered to the British peacefully and with fair terms to the Dutch. It was renamed New York after Charles II's brother.

The eighteenth century saw rapid expansion – the first elementary school in 1696 on Staten Island; the first newspaper in 1725; the first synagogue in 1729; the first theater in 1732; the first college (now Columbia University) in 1754; the first bank in 1784 and the first official census in 1790 when the population numbered thirty-three thousand. At this time, half the white population was English. And the blacks, the 'invisible men of American history', were one fifth of the total. Like Pennsylvania, New York became famous for religious freedom and tolerance. A 1736 view of Manhattan shows six church steeples, each representing a different Protestant observance. Already there was a powerful landed aristocracy and merchant class. Next came a professional class: lawyers, clergy and officials. Then a bulky middle class group of shopkeepers, skilled craftsmen, tavern keepers and small farmers. Then came a group of tenant farmers, hired hands and bond servants, working out a free passage. Last came the slaves, some with a measure of freedom, all pushing strongly in New York towards independence. However Old World the class structure, it was always assumed that an able person might be able to work up to wealth and power. Many did so, and New York history is crammed with their legends.

Then came the War of Independence: nearly one third of all the battles were fought on New York soil. Despite many conflicts of loyalty, New Yorkers believed their state did more than any other to win freedom from British rule. After the peace treaty of 1783, the strongly independent New Yorkers hesitated to join the Union; theirs was the eleventh state to ratify. New York City became the temporary capital of the new nation. And on April 30th, 1789, the people paraded joyously in the streets, and George Washington took the oath of office as first President at Federal Hall – there's a statue to commemorate the great moment.

The nineteenth century saw the makings of the New York we know today. It's hard to believe, but 1819 pictures of City Hall show there were still pigs in the street (critics of the cops, dubbed 'New York's Finest', might say there

still are). The first, settled, lower end of Manhattan grew up like London, in charming, haphazard fashion – perhaps that's why Europeans feel most at home there. Plans for a grid system were made in 1811, and by 1850 the pattern was established that makes Manhattan the easiest city to get about in.

By the time of the American Civil War, the island was built up to today's Forty Second Street; the rest was made up of farms, villages, swamps and shacks made of tar paper and cast off lumber.

The opening of the Erie Canal in 1825 opened up New York to the Great Lakes and the West; by 1840 it was a port second only to London. The city led North America in trade, manufacture, finance – the New York Stock Exchange had started with meetings under button wood trees back in the 1790's. By 1860 the population had hit its first million. In 1899 the population was three million. Today, it's more like eight million.

Change is part of the New York scene. Georgian style houses replaced the Dutch ones, as 'Breetweg' became Broadway. Much re-building took place after a disastrous fire in 1835 destroyed much of the business end of the island. The 1830's saw the elegant houses and squares of the Washington Square area. In 1857 Central Park was conceived by the idealistic Frederick Law Olmsted. Started in a swamp on the city's outskirts 'steeped in the overflow and mush of pigsties, slaughterhouses and bone-boiling works', it turned into a massive public works project that kept four thousand men at work for more than sixteen years. Now it serves as the welcome 'lung' at the heart of Manhattan.

The first elevated railway came in 1868, the first general electricity supplies in 1882 and the first adequate public water supply in 1837 with the building of the Croton Aqueduct. Then in 1883 Brooklyn was joined to Manhattan with an epoch-making feat of engineering, the 6,755 foot long suspension bridge over the East River, precursor of the seventeen bridges and tunnels linking the island to the four boroughs. Brooklyn Bridge was a remarkable achievement then, and is still one of the great sights, staunchly standing up to three times as much traffic as originally envisaged.

Between 1860 and 1890 the fabulous fortunes were made, and the philanthropic rich left their mark on the look of New York. First they competitively built their fantastic town houses, filled them with every treasure money could buy, and then, like Europe's medieval rich easing their consciences by funding lady chapels, the New York rich turned to public buildings. The Frick Museum combines the two. Henry Clay Frick, who made his fortune in Pittsburgh, collected art for forty years. He then built a luxurious town house of 1913 vintage to house it. It was opened to the public in 1935. See it and marvel if you want to taste how the rich lived.

The most stunning examples of what money can do in the right hands must be the Rockefeller Center and the Cloisters. John D. Rockefeller Jr., son of the oil multi-millionaire, planned the former as an act of faith in the

American economy in the dark days after the Wall Street crash of 1929. It comprises twenty-one buildings, mostly of pre-war vintage; gardens, plazas, twenty-five restaurants, and one of the great New York sights, Radio City Music Hall, now teetering on the brink of closure. The Cloisters, another John D. enterprise, put together architectural bits and pieces from all over Europe into a delightful whole, perched on a hill above the Hudson River, in possibly New York's only truly peaceful park.

All through the nineteenth century architects built in a Neo-Classic style (see City Hall) or Victorian Gothic. In 1892 the foundation stone of the 'largest Gothic cathedral in the world' was laid. The Cathedral Church of St John the Divine holds ten thousand worshippers at a time and is still only two-thirds finished today. The style is epitomized in buildings like St Patrick's, started in 1858 in what was then the outskirts, now swallowed up in midtown Manhattan.

It took twentieth century technology to give New York its most characteristic look – the skyscraper – America's unique contribution to the architecture of the world. You can chart the progress of the basic principle. First came the nature of the island itself. Manhattan cannot sprawl – there's nowhere to go but up. Then came the population explosion and rocketing real estate prices at the turn of the century. Next came the precursors – the cast iron front buildings you can see today in SoHo (South of Houston Street). At first building materials wouldn't take high rise strain, so steel and reinforced concrete building methods were devised. After that came the invention and development of elevators and improvements in heating and ventilation. So the sky became the limit. At first the look of the buildings reflected popular styles. Look at the oldest surviving skyscraper – the twenty-story, three-sided Flatiron building, with its bastard Renaissance style. In 1913 came the first super-skyscraper – the sixty-story Woolworth building with its Gothic touches, which kept its record as tallest until 1931.

If you want to see the neck-craning 'canyons of steel' Sinatra sings about in 'Autumn in New York' go to Wall Street. It can make you feel uncomfortably ant-like. Because the closely packed buildings kept light and air from the milling crowds in the narrow street, zoning laws of 1916 dictated a new style; the 'wedding cake' look of successive set back stories. This was absorbed into successful enterprises like the Chrysler Building (1930) and the Empire State (1930, one hundred and two stories high, and still the third tallest building in the world). Since World War Two a new, more elegant style has emerged, inspired by the plan of the Rockefeller Center, completed in 1947. Today's new skyscrapers rise straight up without a break or feature, but are set back from the streets in carefully landscaped plazas, fountain-splashed oases in the concrete jungle. The most beautiful buildings are the work of world famous architects; Gropius designed the Pan Am Building, Saarinen the granite covered CBS Building. Le Corbusier was one of the many with a hand in the Secretariat of the United Nations, a stunningly simple two walls of stone, two of glass, like a narrow box on end; and Mies van der Rohe was responsible for the most beautiful of all, the Seagram Building with its grey glass and bronze panels. No wonder the motto on New York's seal is 'Ever Upward'. Manhattan's skyline is always changing. The latest landmark – and to many eyes the ruin of the Wall Street skyline – are the square twin towers of the World Trade Center, each one a hundred and ten stories high, making them the second tallest buildings in the world. There's an observation deck in one – an elevator whisks you up in fifty-eight seconds – and on a clear day you can see all the way north to Bear Mountain, the most famous peak in the Hudson Highlands, about fifty miles away. It's an ironic thought that crucial to the building and maintenance of the high risers is a colony of Mohawk Indians who live in Brooklyn. Paid off for their tribal lands with a thousand dollars in 1797, they specialize in work at head-turning heights; window washing is a full time job.

The look of New York has been made by alternating graft and philanthropy, idealism and corruption, depression and boom, reform and scandal, near bankruptcy and affluence. New ghettos constantly replace old ones; neighbourhoods prosper and decay. Each phase reflects a new influx of city dwellers. It may be a short history by European standards, but it's packed with human dramas. New York is all about people…and money. And because it's an island, you can see it all, garbage and grandeur, in a simple crosstown walk.

You need a ring of confidence before you get down among the sidewalks of New York. As Police Officer Ann Wilson said (in Vogue, of all places) 'It's a question of walking in a manner that exudes confidence. Yes, if you show fear on the street you are more likely to be victimized.' She also advises you not to carry money; or to carry a small amount in a snatchable purse, and keep the rest tucked away. The rich, it seems, never grubby their fingers with cash, except for taxis, but deal only with credit cards. You have to play it by ear and by intuition; use your wits, turn back if you sense unwelcome, remember that the rowdy streets are the *safe* streets. First, equip yourself with a good map and guide. The green Michelin one is exceptionally clear and interesting. Visit the New York Convention and Visitors Bureau for free information and maps. The big fat Yellow Pages Directory is an eye-opener and entertainment in itself. As they say 'Let your Fingers do the Walking' – use it shrewdly to find where to get what you want – shops, restaurants, services, everything.

Manhattan has to be the world's easiest great city to get about in. Thanks to the grid system (streets go across, avenues go up and down, twenty blocks to the mile) you'll be able to pinpoint or visualize any address with a minimum of practice. Only Broadway, based it seems on an old Indian trail, goes a-winding. Only the area below 14th Street, the oldest, most interesting part of the Island, grew up with an irregular crisscross of named streets on the European plan.

Perhaps a bus tour is a good start – at least it's *safe.* (You can even visit Harlem in a bus. As Bogart rasped in 'Casablanca': 'Well, General, there are some parts of New York you better not try to invade.') The Gray Line company offers a wide variety of round-the-town trips. And the Culture Bus service links museums and other sights. Your ticket lets you get on and off anywhere along the two routes. When you get the feel of the place you can tackle it on public transport, taxi and foot. New Yorkers are biking (the city is flat enough to be fun) and jogging in their thousands. And a brisk walk is often the quickest, most rewarding way between two points. Buses and subways are efficient, if hellish in the rush hour. Both cost 50 cents anywhere – have exact change ready unless you want your first taste of New York invective. The lurid graffiti on the subway trains, is, by the way, being studied as an urban art form! Get a map to find which buses go up or down which Avenue, and which streets have a cross town bus. Transport runs all night, but take a cab if you're unsure. Everyone has a horror tale of what happened while *waiting* for a bus or train.

Cabs, yellow for visibility, are plentiful unless you really want one. Don't expect the cabby to know the city like a London one. Yes, they are like movie characters, and the sound of an unfamiliar accent seems to set each routine in motion. Some are anxious to regale you with pet theories and obsessions; and they expect their personal attention to be reflected in the tip. Others, because of the mugging fear, are separated from you by a thick plate glass window, and money changes hands without any contact.

A stranger in New York will note that there are no apparent public lavatories, no obvious mailboxes.

TOP SIGHTS TO SEE

1. Tall buildings. During your first few days go up to the top of at least one famous tall building and be rendered breathless. You'll get the lay of the land, as well. The old favorite is the Empire State, opened in 1931, still the third tallest. New favorite is the glass-enclosed observation platform on the 107th floor of the World Trade Center tower No. 2; on the proverbial clear day – only a dozen or so a year according to the environment conscious pessimists, New York is an architect's paradise. Take a look at some of the latest, greatest skyscrapers. The Citicorp Center, New York's newest, fifty nine stories above a seven-story, skylighted, tree-dotted atrium incorporating an indestructible church, shops (Britain's Habitat, for one) and restaurants. Or the most hallucinating; the sloping glass curtain wall of '9', West 57th Street, with its crazy criss-cross reflections. Or the Chrysler Building, its distinctive Art Deco overlapping sunburst spire newly polished and gleaming. Each is a triumph of New York nerve.

2. Visit a museum – choose from New York's 48, according to taste. The Metropolitan, with its 234 galleries, is a masterpiece-packed encyclopedia of art, much too much for a casual visit. Pick a section and avoid mental indigestion and chopped-liver feet. For an intimate glimpse of old

masters and beautiful objects in a luxurious home, try the Frick, or the Pierpont Morgan Library. Mr Morgan started collecting autographs as a boy and finished by owning the greatest collection of manuscripts in private hands, which he housed in 1906 and left to the nation in his will. For modern abstract art in a perfect setting try the Guggenheim. Frank Lloyd Wright's revolutionary building was finished in 1959. You take a lift to the top and walk down a top-lit, dazzle-free spiral ramp. For the less abstract sides of modern art, Impressionists to Pop, try the Museum of Modern Art. You'll see the best in modern industrial art from teapots to sewing machines, and classic movies, free, twice a day. Modern Art, however abstract, seems to make sense in New York. Try the Museum of the City of New York for a glimpse of the past. It recreates the city's growth since early times. Audubon Terrace, where the famous bird man used to live, on Broadway between 155th and 156th Streets, is an interesting collection of grand neo-classic buildings including three fascinating museums; The Museum of the American Indian, the Hispanic Society of America, and the American Numismatic Society's history of coinage.

3. Take a boat trip. The Staten Island Ferry runs night and day and costs 25 cents, return free. You'll see the Statue of Liberty on its island and the classically fantastic view of the end of Manhattan. Another idea is a round-the-island trip. There's a three hour long Circle Line boat trip from Pier 83, every forty-five minutes, in the summer. If money's no object you could see Manhattan by helicopter.

4. The Rockefeller Center is a town within a town – a concept in city planning that changed the city's ideas. Every building complex since the War has been influenced. There's a guided tour every forty-five minutes ending with a high speed lift to the 70th floor observation roof of the RCA building. Any visiting American would include a show at Radio City Music Hall, the 6,000 seat Art Deco extravaganza building. The program includes the biggest organ in the world, a symphony orchestra, the Rockettes, thirty long stemmed American beauties kicking in unison, and a movie. Support Radio City! It's always on the edge of closure, possibly because they don't make those family-type movies any more.

5. Visit an ethnic area. Harlem in the 1900's was a clean new neighborhood, and in the 20's *the* place for entertainment; now it's shockingly overcrowded, overpriced, underemployed, and white people are not welcome. It's a bit heart in mouth for many black people too. The Penny Sightseeing Company guarantees you a safe trip. It's salutary to see just why the city is so stressful – that jolt when Fifth Avenue turns from elegant to garbage-clotted after 110th Street. Spanish Harlem scares New Yorkers even more. But no one is scared in Chinatown – on the East Side below Canal Street, where the phone booths have pagoda tops and the food is authentic. Or in Little Italy, North of Canal Street, with its bustling street markets. The Lower East Side street markets on a Sunday are another New York must. While down there remember the latest arty haunt is SoHo (South of Houston Street) which has taken over from the West Village, and the 60's East Village as rents have risen. Chic living will probably do the same to SoHo too. Meantime enjoy!

6. Take a look at older New York. People zoom in on Broadway, and that horrendously tatty midtown section is the great put-off to the sensitive, gaudy with porno movies and massage parlours. Try a refreshingly traditional area like Washington Square (Henry James was born round the corner) and the few remaining stately old early Victorian houses on the North side. The area round Grove Street and Grove Court (tucked away) is made for leisurely Sunday strolling – trees in the streets, a real Manhattan luxury. Urban renewal has its price; only four pre 1776 buildings survive on the island.

7. United Nations Headquarters. Follow the million visitors a year for the guided tour which sets out every fifteen minutes. The Secretariat building is another modern classic, 39 floors of white marble and glass without a break. There are stunning works of art and rooms donated by the different nations, and occasionally you can get a ticket for a UNO debate.

8. The New York Experience. This is a capsule history of New York – an hour-long multi-media and special effects extravaganza with stereo sound, shown in the McGraw Hill building lower plaza. Outside there's a charming reconstruction of a New York street at the turn of the century.

9. The Cloisters. About an hour from Broadway by bus, quicker by subway, you can be in another world – that of the medieval monks. It's an amazing get-away-from-it-all experience if the city begins to get through to you.

10. The Lincoln Center. You can take a culture bug's tour or wander by yourself in this impressive arts conglomerate, set during its 1959-69 construction on fourteen acres of slum (locals, unrehoused, picketed the opening night). There are six splendid buildings to see, plus concerts, opera, ballet, drama to enjoy, free shows at the Guggenheim Band Shell, free films at the branch of the New York Public Library, fabulous works of art and fountains in the various plazas.

11. Central Park. Yes, the grass is trodden thin, half the original trees have gone, the carefully applied top soil has been eroded, but it's still a must if you want to understand New York. They say that since Mayor Lindsay installed more lights, it's been safer (it's still dodgy at night), but many thousands may gather on a summer evening to hear the N.Y. Philharmonic play for free. You can ride a horse, hire roller skates, bike, jog, iceskate in the winter, and see Shakespeare for nothing. There are two zoos, the only open air glamor night spot in the city (the flamboyant, newly done up Tavern on the Green), a mock medieval castle, a Cleopatra's needle – and N.Y.'s equivalent of Peter Pan in Kensington Gardens, a larger than life bronze of Hans Anderson plus an adorable Ugly Duckling.

Flip through the Manhattan phone book and you'll get the idea – New York is the most cosmopolitan city in the world. As Jon Hendricks says, 'It's like looking for a needle in a haystack to find somebody who was born here.' Each wave of immigrants brings a new, special flavour to the melting pot. 1969 clocked up eight million, and with the state's sixteen million, makes it the largest conurbation in the world. And in 1976 one in eight was on welfare.

It's a volatile mix. In 1977 the city's lights went out (imagine the standstill in the most energy consuming area in the world), arson doubled, there was the coldest winter since 1903, the hottest summer day (104 degrees) for 47 years, a psychopathic killer kept the cops on tenterhooks all summer, TV talk show host Stanley Siegal had weekly therapy on camera, and human fly George Willig climbed the south tower of the World Trade Center, was arrested at the top, sued by the City, and eventually fined $1.10 … where else but New York? 'America, you have it better' as the poet Goethe said many years ago. Up to the Declaration of Independence the inhabitants of Manhattan were descendants of the original 200 Dutch families who settled first; some British, some Jews, some black slaves. By 1820 about two out of three residents had Yankee New England forebears. Then, after 1820, the European immigrants began to flow in. By 1855 one fourth of the population was European born, and nearly one half were English, considering themselves the 'aristocrats' of the scene. The Potato Famines of 1846-50 brought the Irish, and by 1890 there were as many as in Dublin. Today, the white line down Fifth Avenue is painted green for the exuberant annual celebrations of St Patrick's Day. Large numbers of Germans came after the abortive 1848 Revolution in their home country and settled round Tomkins Square before moving up to 'Yorkville' round 86th Street, which still has cheerful beerhalls and restaurants with an authentic flavor. There are 325,000 Germans, and four newspapers, plus six radio stations in the language. All were fleeing hard times and unjust politics; the city cast them as craftsmen, businessmen and intellectuals. Large scale Italian immigration started after 1870. Mostly Southern Italians and Sicilians came, working in unskilled trades, but moving into the restaurant, contracting and trucking trades as money was made. Today there are about a million, still deeply attached to the language, with the traditions and fellow feeling of the Old Country. The Chinese, who have always kept themselves to themselves, and are noted for their well behaved, self-disciplining community, came after the Civil War, mostly from Canton. Today there are more than 70,000. The Blacks (the word 'Afro-Americans' sounds perhaps more civil, but 'Black' is sanctioned by their own usage these days) were among the first New Yorkers. The slave market closed and freedom was given to children on reaching adulthood in 1799. Huge numbers arrived from the South at the beginning of the century, and also from the Caribbean islands. Today one fifth of New Yorkers are black. There's always a new under-dog – and the latest is the Puerto Rican: in 1910 there were about 500. Mass immigration began after the Second World War, and today there are more than 610,000, which gives a distinct Latin flavor to the city. There are more Jews than in Israel and the culture – particularly a way of speaking Anthony Burgess calls 'Yidglish' – is the way New Yorkers talk. 'In New York, *everyone's* a Jew', Lenny Bruce said – more or less. There are tens of thousands of Greeks, Romanians, Scandinavians, and, of course, the population of Manhattan *doubles* every day, as people come in to work.

Each wave of immigrants paid its dues, and had its special hard time establishing itself, by starting at the bottom and rising up the prosperity ladder. Some of the abrasive banter, the snappy comebacks and energetic abuse, is survival talk, a definition of status. There's always a stranger in town; last week *you* were the stranger. Hence the extraordinary hospitality extended to the new face, the startling surface candor of the conversation – intimate details on the flimsiest acquaintance; the emphasis on the up to date; the reliance on status symbols to define self and assess others' place in the scheme of things. Hence, according to anthropologist Margaret Mead, the emphasis on hygiene – a motley crowd crammed together, eating varied foods, made bearable by deodorants and mouthwash. Hence also the brainwashing of fashion – slang, hobbies, people, looks, taken up, then dropped with great rapidity. In a classless society, money does the talking. And in New York, you can turn *anything* into money if you can figure an angle. This gives the city its particular edge and particular desperation – take a trip to the West Side or the Bowery to see how far you could sink if you don't keep making the right money. The theoretical safety net of the Welfare State isn't there. Desperation makes everyone edgy; every door is multi-locked, never opened to a stranger; every cab driver sees you *inside* your building before he goes off, every New Yorker tells you a tale of the man standing next to him in the elevator hitting him on the head for a wallet.

Technology has made life in Manhattan possible. Every day the Sanitation Department takes 23,000 tons of rubbish from the five boroughs. The summer is steamily, unbearably hot. Clothes turn to wet rags when you walk a block. In the poor parts without air conditioning everyone sits in the street, and the kids splash in the turn-on fire hydrants – the poor man's Plaza fountain. You drink endless ice water, take three showers a day, go indoors for a breath of cool air. In the winter snow piles up in ten foot drifts, the poor freeze to death on doorsteps. Best times to visit are the long, golden autumn, or you might try to hit the erratic, heavenly spring, but money buys any comfort you like – another motivation to make it. Make it and you make it easier for yourself every day, in every way. No one can afford to be content. If you make it in New York, you can make it anywhere; and every working day another immigrant arrives, determined to make it.

Hollywood apart (and it ain't what it used to be), New York is the entertainment capital of America. And how the other important big cities hate that. Each has a symphony orchestra, ballet company, opera house – but New York is where the prestigious critics are and where the reputations are made. It's the place where both the lively and straightfaced arts come to show themselves. No visit to New York is complete without a sampling, according to your tastes. Mark your choice in one of the weeklies – the <u>New Yorker</u>, <u>New York</u>, <u>Cut</u>, <u>The Village Voice</u>, or the <u>New York Times</u> (its 10lb Sunday edition covers everything…though as <u>New York</u> says tartly 'One ought to remember, however, that some aspects of life can and should be lived without the guidance of this newspaper'). There's an embarrassment of riches – but some of the arts are peculiarly New York…

The Broadway Show – perhaps the 'Great White Way' as the hub of show biz is a myth these days…only 30 theaters left in the erstwhile 'theater district'. And the cost of a night out with taxis, dinner, drinks and seats at a hit show could cost an average week's wage. However, the thing to see is the 'Musical' – every season there's a hit show – that unique, expert blend of song, story, dance and spectacle which only America pulls off to perfection. Off-Broadway has taken over much of the serious theater with the less lavish budget. And Off-Off Broadway has taken the experimental end, where off-beat staging in lofts, living room size places, can take chances. The work can be solid to wilfully shocking. There's always the hit show in these areas too.

Dance – the culture hero of the age is the male dancer, says New York magazine. New York has every kind of dance. From the Balanchine classics in the repertoire of the New York City Ballet, at Lincoln Center, through the modern dance companies of Alvin Ailey, Paul Taylor, Alwin Nikolais (the costume is the action), Twyla Tharp, to shoe string companies in lofts and church halls, all making a virtue of idiosyncrasy, the traditions old and new are alive and kicking, in the very best of hands. Then there's the pioneer company, the Dance Theater of Harlem, masterminded by Arthur Mitchell, Balanchine's first black dancer, with its classical and neo-classical repertoire and training school. American dancers have unique qualities as classical dancers; they're beautiful, competitive, with glittering techniques, but the fun and invention is in the native styles, tap and popular dancing from the streets and ballrooms, 'modern' from the pathbeating work of Martha Graham and the 'thirties innovators. 'Dance Magazine' has news and views.

Movies – New Yorkers see the movie classics over and over – can quote you scenes that have become part of the life style. 'Revival Houses' are listed lovingly with full descriptions of the movie classics in the 'New Yorker'. See the listings for classic revivals at various New York museums, too. Porno movies have their styles and classics too. 42nd Street is the street, plenty of action inside and outside the cinemas, if that's your thing. Here your nose is rubbed in another side of New York life – the neon-bright day and dreadful night of New York's freakies.

The American Song Book – an entertainment perfected by a handful of polished, beloved performers generally described as 'with impeccable repertoires'. A piano player or singer-player makes a reputation with a knowledge of the offbeat classics of the American popular song – the lesser known works of Gershwin, Arlen, Porter… the songs that were dropped during the out of town tryouts, salvaged from shows that didn't survive past Saturday. The range and the audience are selective. It's one of the few forms of nostalgia New York permits itself. Singers who specialise in the recherché seldom travel – names like Mabel Mercer, Bobby Short, Blossom Dearie are ones to conjure with; and the settings, so-called piano bars, are perfect for this bitter-sweet pleasure – the intimate, the wry, the city inspired.

Jazz – 'Jazz is America's classical music' says Billy Taylor, leader of the Jazzmobile enterprise which has taken famous jazz musicians to the deprived streets of the city for more than fourteen years. Jazz is back as a popular attraction, thanks possibly to the annual Newport in New York event each July – when every concert hall in town seems to be swinging and there's music in the streets, too. There's nothing like the sight and sound of a saxophone player, such as the fantastic George Adams, releasing a sudden *cry* which reverberates off the glass and steel about him to feel the sound of New York, and the voice of its people. As the late jazz great Rahsaan Rolad Kirk said, 'New York is one of a kind – it throws everything back at you.'

As Neil Simon says 'New York, you're a fun city.' Maybe it's because New York only becomes really beautiful, really glamorous after dark, but night life is another New York tradition. Maybe there's that special charge of energy, like the little jab of static you get off the doorknobs, that lets New Yorkers play as hard as they work. After dark is a vocation, a whole industry.

Fashion is the thing. There's always the latest place where they're fighting to get in. Next season it's deader than King Tut.

Discotheques. There's always the disco of the season – tonight it's Studio 54 'every star in the world turns up sooner or later' (on the opening night Sinatra couldn't get in). The owner looks you over at the door, and if he doesn't like what he sees, you don't get in, whoever you are. Latest twist is the basement addition; you're nobody unless you can get in, *and* get into the basement. Then there's Régine's glamorous outpost on Park Avenue, an amazing pink on plum, plus silver, Art Deco interior with the latest in artfully presented 'cuisine minceur' to tempt the rich slimmer.

Singles Bars 'where romance dares you,' according to the Yellow Pages. Here's another New York specialty, with disturbing overtones, nastily underlined in the movie 'Looking for Mr Goodbar'. There are, it's said, a million smart, bright, unattached girls on the upper East Side. Girls with great teeth, clean hair, shapely legs, talkative with the latest slang, all complaining that New York is full of homosexuals. They're demanding… 'Men are to buy you cocktails,' insists Helen Gurley Brown, editor of 'Cosmopolitan', and they're looking for Mr Right in the

singles bars, while the singles bars are full of men looking for a quick lay. So the atmosphere is predatory, rough on the sensitive and the romantic. Names like Tuesday's, Wednesday's, Thursday's, Friday's are the usual ones. Again, fashion is all.

Cocktail Bars. Despite the news that Perrier is the smartest drink, New York fostered the cocktail back in the '20s so anyone could absorb hard liquor between meals – New Yorkers still tend to drink before rather than serve wine *with*. (Some New Yorkers even associate wine with deadbeats.) The names of the classics; Manhattans, Highballs, Martinis, Daiquiris, Old Fashioneds, are part of social history but all are ways of making a slug of the hard stuff more or less palatable, but the cocktail bar and the cocktail hour (that magic moment when the blue of the dusk meets the gold of the Scotch) is pure New York. Watch all the lights come on from the top of a tall building – it's real, urban enchantment. It's a budget-y way of enjoying the ambience of a smart place at the lowest cost.

Jazz. It sometimes shocks European jazz lovers, raised on recorded reputations to find an idol treated as part of the wallpaper in a bar or club. New Yorkers take their jazz talents for granted. You can go to a plush wine and dine place like the Rainbow Room and find yourself dancing to a band including enough star names to make a fan gasp – and playing waltzes and tangos. Pit bands of Broadway shows are studded with jazz greats; a culture hero may be playing in the corner of a crowded – or empty – little bar. It's a depressing fact of a jazzman's life, yet it's a wonderful thing to hear the music in the New York setting – the legendary older survivors like Roy Eldridge still have their skills and spirit intact, and the avant garde sounds right here – overstated in its rage elsewhere. The so-called 'loft' scene is a refreshing new idea, part of the arty move to SoHo. Converted warehouses, sometimes homes or art galleries by day, become informal premises at night where you sit about (on the floor if you like) and hear the real thing, at the experimental end of the jazz spectrum. Musician owned places like Ali's Alley (owned by drummer Rashied Ali), Studio Rivbea (owned by saxophone player Sam Rivers and his wife) and so on, aim to cut out the exploitative or indifferent middle man and get the music straight to the people who want to hear it. Possibly the music is better than the attendance; as usual with jazz reputations the European fans have picked up these vibes before New York.

Phone 'Jazzline' for up to date news on who's playing where. It's a daily recorded bulletin.

Nightclubs – still part of the New York mythology. Some legendary names are being taken up again, brushed off and re-introduced – names like the Stork Club (a white on white 'thirties fantasy) the Cotton Club (the great Harlem name of the 'thirties), the King Cole bar at the St Regis, with its now historic Maxfield Parrish mural, are all past glories given a touch of artificial respiration. Some of the old stalwarts still claim their fans; El Morocco, with its zebra striped banquettes, the Copacabana promising 'a nite to remember, with unlimited liquor, and full filet mignon dinner.'

New Yorkers seem to like their nightclubs well bred – it's touching how they hanker after what they call 'class', in a country that prides itself on not having any. The great hotels have super food, super service, super surroundings and superstars to entertain. Dressing up is de rigeur. A posh disco like The Library at the Barbizon Plaza states 'No denim, gentlemen required to wear jackets.' At more modest levels there are the clubs like Catch a Rising Star, that features continuous hopefuls; The Improvisation, which has comics and singing waitresses. You can still dance to two live bands (Count Basie's maybe) at the Roseland. You can still taste the flavor of the sixties at the last surviving Village coffee house and listen to folkie entertainment. You can drink at New York's oldest bar, McSorley's which banned women up to the 'seventies, true to its 1854 traditions. You can hear the best eclectic pop in town at the Bottom Line. The night is young.

Disorient yourself by eating something totally unfamiliar – New York's the place to do it. It's part of the fun; the great gastronomic experience at a posh, pricey place; the restaurant in the New Yorker cartoon 'So So Restaurant …Acceptable Food;' down to the day-old food free at the back of the Horn and Hardart automat. Wherever you come from, you can find a facsimile of your native cuisine; whatever you fancy you'll find in the Yellow Pages. You don't even need to step out; just 'Dial a Steak' to Beefsteak Charlie's.

Elegance. New Yorkers equate elegant eating with French cuisine – the most prestigious, expensive restaurants are places like Lutèce, La Grenouille (where the Beautiful People lunch and check each other out), Le Pavillon, Voison. The latest name to add is Le Relais, and the latest taste thrill the non-fattening 'cuisine minceur'. If you want a taste of luxury you might make your main meal lunch, the prices are significantly easier.

The elegant hotels have elegant restaurants. You might investigate the piazza restaurants of the famous skyscrapers – Citicorp has eleven; nine nationalities from English to rotisseried venison. Or you might try the top of a tower, like The Windows on the World at the World Trade Center. New Yorkers like to make eating an *event.*

The decor wins in many famous restaurants. Greatest idea; the Four Seasons in the beautiful Seagram building, which changes waiters' garb, flowers, upholstery, napkins, matchboxes, ashtrays, plates and food with the seasons of the year. Add in the works of art that decorate the place and the French food and you've got something – including a bill. There's O'Henry's, an old favourite in an old butcher's shop. Serendipity which combines an antique shop, a spiffy (favorite New York word) gift shop and a restaurant. There's The Grand Cafe, all Art Deco. Any New Yorker will tell you the latest place where the people 'ooh' and 'aah'.

Italian. The great Italian restaurants are less expensive than the French ones, right down to the pizza slices you pick up on a street corner. The best loved is Mamma Leone's 'Where strong appetites are met and conquered.'

Steak. Steak used to be the American obsession – people thought they'd *die* without a daily stomachful. Now, with the cholesterol scare, they're not so sure. Visit East 45th Street for steak places, all on the expensive side. You can still get obscenely large slabs of meat at places like Bruno's Pen and Pencil. 'The Right People come to the Pen and Pencil; forty years serving America's steak connoisseurs,' and take away your leftovers in a doggie bag. Then there's the mass production method of the Tad chain – identical charcoal cooked steak while you wait.

To see and be seen. Many restaurants turn eating into a ritual public event. Elaine's; Sardi's (theatrical first nights are nail-biting time here as the cast waits for the morning paper reviews); the Russian Tea Room, which is chic, show-off and noisy; the Ginger Man which is handy for the Lincoln Center set. New York never stops. If the thought of an all night eatery un-nerves you look at the Brasserie which caters to the top end of the subculture. It's in the ultra chic Seagram Building and it never closes; a steak and a bottle of wine at three a.m. will cost you about twenty dollars.

Sea food. Another New York superlative, fresh seafood is close by and is a must for the diet conscious; oysters, striped bass, king crab legs, clam chowder, oyster stew, lobsters and bay scallops are all fresh and fine. Old favorite places are: Sweet's, famous for simple, perfect cooking of the freshest fish (it's a serious place and closes smartly at 8 p.m.); the Oyster Bar in Grand Central Station which serves nothing but clams and oysters; and the biggest is Paddy's Clam House which serves two to three thousand people a day, at paper covered tables, in a cheap, huge, bustling place.

Brunch is another American classic – it's Mom's Sunday treat – means a meal anytime between 10 a.m. and 4 p.m. Try the specialties; pancakes, waffles, eggs and bacon or steaks washed down with Sangria and Bloody Marys, or even champagne. And at The Cookery you can have jazz with your brunch.

Soul food. This is almost unknown outside America – the food of the deep South. Try fried chicken (Kentucky Fried chicken from the takeout is an approximation), ham hocks, chitterlings, fried pork chops, ribs, collard greens and black-eyed peas, hot corn bread, sweet potato pie, fried corn and candied yams. All rich and indigestable, yet filling!

Ice cream. A must for anyone who remembers old movies with the teenagers licking away at huge sundaes and sodas. Nowadays the smart New Yorker is into frozen yogurt – fewer calories, you know, but you can still get the classics: at the Howard Johnson chain, famous for its 27 varieties of ice cream; at Rumpelmayer's, which is staid and old world elegant with mirrors and mosaic columns, at Peppermint Park, with 32 homemade flavors, and at Hick's, with its custom made sodas. Schrafft's – the famous chain – seems to be in a tatty decline, though the ices are still good –

those ices still scream America to the outside world.

Fast food. New Yorkers tend to eat on the run during the working day. There are the hamburger chains; Brew Burger, Burger Bistro, Burger King, Mcdonald's – everyone knows just what to expect. You can also eat fast Mexican (Taco Rico), fast Japanese (Chick Teri), fast Jewish (Bagel Nosh), fast German (Zum Zum). The Chock Full o' Nuts chain is bland tastewise but clean as a whistle.

Far Eastern food. Chinese food – the greatest cuisine in the world, some say – has been part of New York since early days – Chinatown is still the place to go. The big boom in recent years, with the craze for less lavish, low cholesterol diets, has been for Japanese food. Tempura (freshly fried vegetables and sea food in light batter), sashimi (finely-sliced raw fish), yakitori (broiled skewerfuls of meat or seafood) and sushi bars (offering seaweed-wrapped rice) are all part of the ritual. Japanese soup with noodles is another warming, filling dish. You can find Japanese restaurants at every price range (mostly upper), and a self service, at Genroku Sushi, on Fifth Avenue. You watch the conveyor belt and help yourself. If you want to experiment, as a first timer, the prices are reasonable. Look about and you'll find every kind of Far Eastern cuisine – Korean, Thai, Philippine; all the varieties of Chinese.

Delicatessen. Jewish food is known as dairy food – strictly kosher and hearty vegetarian (these days there are kosher pizza palaces and even a kosher Chinese restaurant) and deli. The largest deli in the world is Katz's on Houston Street, another famous Lower East side name is Ratner's, a strictly no-meat place. Here's a quote from an ad. that's typical of the vocational pride of the New York restaurateur; 'Other restaurants sell you ground liver and have the audacity to call it chopped liver. Even my mother in law compliments me on my chopped liver.' Visit 156 Second Avenue for the real thing.

Latin American. Tacos, tostados, enchiladas, tamales, chili beans and rice – earthy and spicy; here is another New York taste to try. You can get a combination plate of everything at Mañana. Or look out for the subtleties they say exist – Tex-Mex, Cuban, Brazilian, Chilean, Puerto Rican, Latin-Chinese, Venezuelan, Dominican – and forget the horrors like spiced chicken in chocolate sauce.

This has to be Paradise for the person with money burning a hole in the pocket book…the streets present constant temptation. The great wits of the city are devoted to the art of selling – what's Madison Avenue *for*? Wit is not absent – the pun is not dead – with jewelry shops named 'The Carat Patch' or 'The Venerable Bead'; a secondhand toy shop called 'Play It Again'; a secondhand gown shop 'Gently Worn Inc.' ('when frugal got to be fun'); a quilt shop called 'Down With Love'; shops called 'Shoe Biz' and 'The Forgotton Woman' ('for well endowed chic') and a plastic shop called 'Perplexity'.

Certain aspects of shopping are uniquely New York.

The department store. The success of the last few years has been the renaissance of Macy's – the great classic department store which everyone took for granted,

because though the prices were right the image had become ho-hum (as they say). It's had a face lift and is now back in favor. Macy's Parade on Thanksgiving Day is a tradition that's part of New York – it means Christmas is really coming, and the statistics are staggering. Five million customers a year; furniture departments (1,000 armchairs to choose from), so football-field big you have to phone an assistant; staff speaking forty languages; 218 model rooms to look at, plus an entire fully furnished house; two acres of children's things, including a 'lovable new pet shop'; thirty butchers as a for-instance in the vast food department; the biggest fabric department in the city; the world's biggest linens department; prices from top to the grabbing throngs round the bargain tables on the main floor; Macy's could do you proud from the cradle to the grave. Gimbel's, its next door rival, still goes on claiming 'Nobody, but Nobody Undersells Gimbels.'

Each famous store has its own image, its own devotees:

Bloomingdales ('My God, they're so *chic* at Bloomie's') is the only complete store on the Upper East side, so caters to the rich young marrieds and the swinging singles. Everything is imaginative, unexpected and eye catching, the windows verging on the kinky. The specials; the latest must-have bit of nonsense; the 'homescape' range of furnishings, everyone goes to buy the latest decorating look from the 27 famous model rooms. Bloomie's sells a total look, a life style that makes you feel you must be right.

Lord and Taylor goes in for the elegantly youthful – not too staid or too faddish. It's Fifth Avenue's oldest store and famous for its total visual presentation. **B. Altman** is the most conservative store, strong on traditional values including exclusive reproductions of American traditional furniture.

Henri Bendel is perhaps the most stunning – stroll round its main floor street of tiny, exclusive boutiques. It's only for the rich…and the slim (no clothes above size twelve), whilst **Bergdorf Goodman** has the heaviest luxury.

Sak's Fifth Avenue says 'our job is to be editors of fashion'. **Bonwit Teller** is famous for designing clothes and the Finale Shop, an end of season bonanza from all departments. **Orbach's** is famous for budget versions of French couture. **Korvette's** has had a rapid rise to fame as a discount merchandise supermarket.

America invented 'sportswear' as a general term for what the average American woman lives in – elegant but simple separates and co-ordinates, at all price levels. The look is eptomized in the great American classic, the shirtwaist dress – the pioneer's calico brought up-to-date each season. Then the casual – the great American denims; the pantsuit – American sportswear borrows heavily from Europe – when it wants to be elegant. Thrift shops, known elegantly as 'resale shops' are still a rage if you want to buy old-fashioned craftsmanship at the price you'd pay for polyester.

Snob Shopping. Many New Yorkers would thank you more for a gold toothpick in a Tiffany box than a mink from Macy's. Status is all. Still, it costs you nothing to look.

And you might join the 'Saturday Stroll' up Madison Avenue from 57th to 86th Streets, checking out the smartest and most exclusive shops all the way – or the status shops twelve blocks up Fifth Avenue from the new Olympic Towers – watching the rich greet each other – ending at Parke-Bernet where the classiest antique auctions are held (it's a way of life for antique-knowing New Yorkers), then across to Lexington and back in time for afternoon tea at the Plaza. Everything you wear, everything you do, everything you buy, can be interpreted by the status seekers, for or against you, in the scheme of things.

Good New York buys. Visit the museum shops: the New York Public Library, Museum of City of New York, Whitney Museum and the Metropolitan, for reproductions of treasures, crafts, jewellery, toys and games. Pick posters and graphics; easy to pack and store; shops like Park South Gallery at Carnegie Hall, Gallery II (graphics) Poster Originals (contemporary Art posters) Associated American Artists' Gallery for signed originals in woodcuts, etchings, lithos, etc. Linens – most of the name designers, Blass, de La Renta, Donghia and so on design for manufacturers like Martex, Wamsutta, Fieldcrest. Everything from the pretty, the dramatic, the subliminal (the famous sheet set with 'Sleep, Sleep, Sleep' all over it), the childlike, is printed on a sheet these days. Again, they make good gifts and lightweight packing. Records; the place has to be Sam Goody's: four Manhattan branches, specializing in discount buys, but the record scene is vast and specialized. Discount books; Marboro Books, specialists in discount books and posters; Barnes and Noble, which provides supermarket baskets for your finds. Gadgets; Hammacher Schlemmer is the place for American ingenuity. Dancewear; 'Danskins are not just for Dancing' says the slogan and all the famous names like Capezio have extended their styles and colors to tempt the ordinary woman as well as the figure-conscious dieter or budding ballerina. Today leotards and tights are the smart girl's underwear or the basis for many styles of dressing. You might look at Azuma branches for the gay, cheap, throwaway 'must have' home accessory; the Singer Sewing Center or the classic 'Five and Ten' for 'notions' – the gadget you didn't know existed and didn't know you needed till you saw it; Party Bazaar for an amazing range of colorful 'everything in paper' party and picnic things; New York Exchange for Women's Work for Handicrafts.

Each and every New Yorker is proud of knowing exactly where, and only where, the best of everything can be found. So pick brains…

Sunday is New York's more or less peaceful time – no one's rushing in or out of the island – time to stroll (Central Park is closed to car traffic), time to sit and enjoy what little green places are grudgingly provided in the midst of the concrete jungle.

From midday to early evening you could cool off in the fountain court of the Frick Museum when it's summer hot outside – in winter there are chamber music concerts. And there's a lovely garden next door. The Museum of Modern Art has a famous Sculpture Garden with a cafeteria, fountains, marble pavings, trees, and music on summer evenings. You can get an indoor-outdoor feeling in the winter too. Eat at Christy's Skylite Gardens; a super glasshouse with trees and everything, even when the snow is falling. Or Olympic Place, inside the newish Olympic tower, a landscaped indoor park with leafy trees and a waterfall.

It's classic to dine out by the Rockefeller fountains on summer nights. Newer, perhaps, is the lavish Tavern on the Green in Central Park. Or The River Cafe, New York's only floating restaurant on the Brooklyn side of the East River.

Apart from Central Park, the park space in New York is scanty and sought after. Paley Park, only reachable through the shopping arcade on East 53rd Street, is a new one, tiny but tempting, with a twenty foot waterfall, trees, vines and space to sit out. Friendship Garden is another pocket size oasis, shady, quiet and hidden away behind gates at 652 Lexington Avenue. Kids splash in the Washington Square fountain, while their parents sit out under the venerable trees and listen to the impromptu folk singing. Bryant Park is Midtown's oasis, sycamore shaded and with piped music to entertain the bevies of sandwich-munching office workers. The post-war skyscraper complexes have carefully considered plazas around the base, where the plash of fountains gives a feeling of coolness when the temperature soars – New Yorkers go there and pant. Uptown there's nowhere like Fort Tryon Park; you'll feel miles from the hustle of the city's heart. It's hilly, overlooking the Hudson and has a choice little botanic garden, peaceful and green – you don't see too much green in New York apart from St Patrick's Day!

When the heat gets unbearable New Yorkers make for the beaches. Nearest are Coney Island (more famous for its fairground than its peace) and Jones Beach where you can find a personal patch of beach along the twelve miles of magnificent sand and breakers, little more than an hour's drive from the city. Farther afield, but no more than three hours away, are the thirty-five public beaches of Long Island. You can stay home and swim, however. The Henry Hudson Hotel, among others, has a pool. Swim for free if you stay at the City Squire Motor Inn, Loew's Midtown Inn or in the roof pool at the Sheraton Motor Inn.

Staten Island – on the ferry or by car on the Verrazano-Narrows Bridge – is one big, almost undiscovered oasis. Clove Lakes Park and the well-kept Von Briesen Park are the native's well-kept secrets. There's a zoo, smallish but with the best reptile collection in the States. And a conservation area at High Rock Park which is being carefully preserved in its natural state. There's an attractive village at Richmondtown in the process of restoration and, in the midst of beautiful gardens, the Jacques Marchais Center of Tibetan Art – a unique collection. Staten Island has never been fashionable and is consequently semi unspoilt, with uncrowded beaches all along the south-eastern shore. It's the proverbial breath of fresh air; a taste of rural Americana and only half an hour on the ferry from Manhattan.

It is possible, in Central Park, to gain some idea of the terrain of Manhattan before the city was built. Great outcrops of rock still jut out from the thousands of tons of topsoil that were used to landscape the park. Central Park occupies an area of some 840 acres from 59th to 110th Streets and from Fifth Avenue to Central Park West.

This is a rustic haven right in the heart of Manhattan where anyone can go about the business of doing exactly what they want to do, from energetic pursuits to the distinctly lethargic.

Symbol of a nation and an ideal, the Statue of Liberty left welcomes visitors to New York.

Central Park can be different things to different people. There is, of course, noise and brashness and there is the color of balloon sellers' wares and the crowds around the boating lake, but there are also the quiet aspects; the soaring structures that go to make up Manhattan *overleaf* reflected, along with the trees and the blue sky, in the tranquil waters of a lake *left*.

The hansom cabs that ply their trade in and around Central Park were first operated by London cab drivers who found themselves out of employment at home due to the coming of the motor car. They came to New York in search of work and their way of life remains unchanged to this day *above*.

Snow can lend enchantment to any scene, and this is particularly so in Central Park. The park, normally drab in winter, like any other park, suddenly comes to life as people enjoy winter pursuits such as ice-skating, skiing or an impromptu game of ice hockey.
All around are the skyscrapers, which leave one in no doubt that this is still the heart of New York.

Photographed from New Jersey, across the Hudson River, the skyline of Manhattan overleaf twinkles with thousands of lights.

Most people like the prettiness of the idea of snow, and it certainly softens harsh outlines and lends a different aspect to whatever it touches. Going about one's daily business in a city that is almost brought to a standstill by heavy snow is far from fun, however. Streets flanked by high buildings can become canyons, down which the snow is blown top left in a blizzard-like fury.

Drifting snow is cleared from around the Gothic structure of St. Patrick's Cathedral center left and road works are abandoned in the extreme weather above as are vehicles below, and a rare taxi becomes a much-sought-after prize below left.

Pedestrians make their way carefully across roads now made treacherous, while the skier right is enough to make people rub their eyes in disbelief.

Right in the heart of Manhattan, opposite St. Patrick's Cathedral, stands what is considered to be one of the architectural marvels of New York, Rockefeller Center. The land on which the complex is built still, in fact, belongs to Columbia University, to whom it was left by Dr. David Hosack, and as a reminder that it is not a public street, Rockefeller Plaza is closed to traffic once every year.

The most impressive approach to Rockefeller Center is from Fifth Avenue, through the Channel Gardens left, planted, according to season, with a changing variety of flowers, and at the end of which lies the sunken plaza, a skating rink in winter, above left, and a restaurant in summer previous page. Behind the plaza stands Paul Manship's huge, golden statue of Prometheus right and, behind that, the soaring façade of the RCA Building above.

On Fifth Avenue stands the statue of Atlas below, with, on his shoulders, a symbolic representation of the earth.

Summer rain cools the city streets and brings into play a variety of weather protection. There are plastic rain hats and there are doorways to shelter in, of course, and there are large, serviceable umbrellas, fashionably-shaped ones, obviously borrowed ones and those chosen to complement an outfit. Taxis are suddenly in great demand where, only a few minutes previously, people were happy to walk in the sunshine. Showers are usually only temporary interruptions to summer days, however, and not to be taken too seriously.

Rockefeller Center's sunken plaza serves as a popular skating rink in winter overleaf.

36

Fifth Avenue is synonymous with elegant shopping, expensive limousines and everything that goes with that particular life-style. It represents retail selling brought to a fine art; the names, the shop windows and the goods all act as inducements to buy. Not all the people who hurry along its sidewalks are shoppers, however. The skyscrapers house the offices of many of the world's most prestigious companies, all crowded with workers who commute from all parts of the city and beyond.

The exterior of St. Patrick's Cathedral right is based on Cologne Cathedral and the interior derives from the cathedral at Amiens, in France. In almost any other setting in the world St. Pat's, as St. Patrick's Cathedral is affectionately known, would dwarf, in its neo-Gothic splendor, its surroundings, but this is not so in New York.

Ever part of the New York scene, the city's familiar 'yellow cabs' are shown overleaf.

New York's skyscrapers are many and varied. Most of the newer ones are severely angular, unlike the decorative Chrysler Building, the top of which may be seen below left. This was the first building to use metal – in this case stainless steel – as a facing material.

Although it has now been superseded as the tallest skyscraper in the world, nevertheless the Empire State Building top left, above, below and right *remains a very special structure; the epitome of the skyscraper. It contains 102 stories and the tip of its television tower reaches a height of 1,472 feet above sea level.*

Over one and a half million visitors are attracted to it each year and they find it enough to say that they have visited the Empire State Building, rather than the current record holder for the world's tallest. The Empire State Building stands on the site once occupied by the old Waldorf Astoria Hotel. Construction started on St. Patrick's Day, 1929 and it was completed in 1931 but, because of the Stock Market crash and the subsequent fall in real estate values, it stood almost empty until World War II.

EMPIRE STATE

Thanksgiving Day, celebrated throughout the U.S., on the fourth Thursday in November was originally instituted in the autumn of 1621 by the Massachusetts Bay governor, William Bradford, who invited neighboring Indians to join the Pilgrims in a three-day festival to give thanks for the harvest and other blessings of the past year. Officially proclaimed a national holiday in 1863, by President Lincoln, this special day is traditionally feasted with turkey and pumpkin pie and, in New York, provides a very good reason for indulging in yet another parade.

Clowns and acrobats, famous television personalities and stalwart bands provide fun and amusement, while the plea from Macy's representatives *right* appears to be "don't rain on my parade...."

Densely-packed Manhattan is shown overleaf from the top of the Empire State Building.

Almost all of America's major companies have contributed to modern Manhattan's architecture. Outside the General Motors Building on Fifth Avenue a plaza has been provided right where it is possible to sit in the sunshine and enjoy a break from the city's crowded sidewalks.

Street entertainers, an advertisement-covered bus, a policeman on traffic duty and a hansom cab decorated with flowers all go to make up the ever-changing and fascinating face of New York.

The elegant façade below is that of the Public Library.

50

"The snow is snowing, the wind is blowing…" and the city streets lie buried under a layer of crisp, white snow, softening the outlines of the mass of concrete and steel buildings as they rise to meet the swollen sky. Yet, while traffic and citizens find the conditions hazardous and the arduous task of clearing the thoroughfares is painstakingly carried out, New York's younger citizens happily contemplate, in their own 'winter wonderland', the figures made possible by this unusually heavy fall – a trio of gaily be-decked snowmen.

To 'make it' on Broadway, in a resounding hit, is probably one of the major ambitions of most actors and actresses, This internationally known theater-land is the hub of New York's entertainment world and some of the most ambitious musicals and plays ever produced have been performed in the theaters within the Broadway area. Broadway's excitement is almost tangible, seen in a blaze of lights at Times Square overleaf.

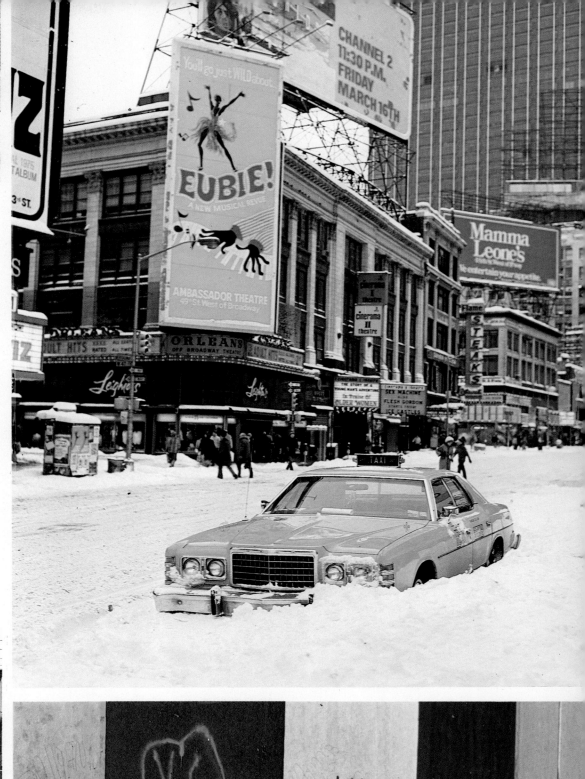

53

The outsize, inflatable characters of Kermit the Frog *left* and Snoopy *right* appear to fill the space between the skyscrapers and add an incongruous note to Macy's Thanksgiving Day Parade.

While high-stepping soldiers of Minnesota's Marching Ambassadors *above* step out in unison between the jostling crowds lining the sidewalks, the marchers *below*, with proudly displayed banners held aloft, keep time in style, for not even the rain can dampen the enthusiasm of the annual event of this very special Thanksgiving Day Parade.

Overleaf, a bewildering plethora of signs illuminate world-famed 42nd Street.

Chinatown – streets packed with traffic and people; distinctive pagoda-like telephone booths; tempting restaurants and irresistible shops – yet amid the bustle there is always time to catch up on the news or grab a quick snack – Chinese style, in cosmopolitan New York overleaf.

Greenwich Village this page, famed for its old Bohemian atmosphere, is a charming village community with a fascinating array of craft and curio shops, coffee-houses and bistros, restaurants and art galleries. Bounded on all sides by commercial establishments, Greenwich Village is unique, for unlike the rest of the city with its broad, straight boulevards, the haphazard streets of the Village meander and criss-cross in an enigmatic maze. Its center of activity is in Washington Square, where the residents gather to play chess, talk, or just 'watch the world go by'.

Today the quaint, remodeled houses have once again become expensive homes for the rich, yet the area still retains its charming 'artiness', evocative of Montmartre in Paris, with its numerous open-air cafés, restaurants and night clubs.

From Brooklyn, the twinkling lights of Lower Manhattan can be seen overleaf.

Stanford White's famous Washington Arch *right stands regally in this renowned Square of Greenwich Village. Sketching, music-making and quiet, absorbing games above, can all be enjoyed in this hub of Village community life.*

Night transforms Manhattan's skyline, reflected in the water, overleaf.

As the day progresses the streets around Wall Street *right* teem with office-workers scurrying about their business: past marble fronted buildings *below* and the New York Stock Exchange *above*.

Patriotism personified – the 'Uncle Sam' personality *left*, resplendent in red, white and blue – hawks his flags on the streets of New York.

The clean, sleek lines of Manhattan are seen by day *overleaf* from the promenade on Brooklyn Heights.

BROWN BROTHERS HARRIMAN & Co.

59 WALL ST.

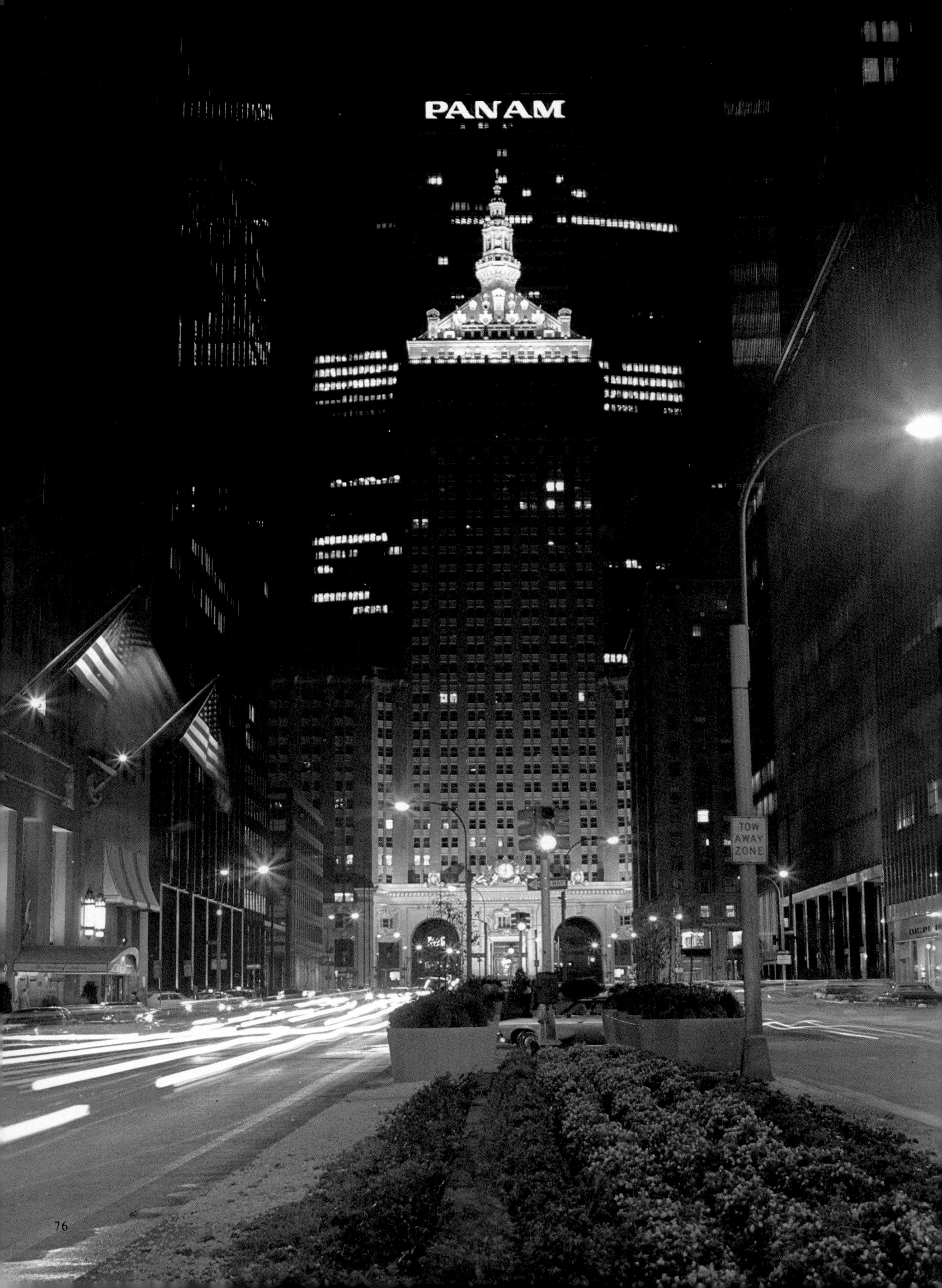
PANAM
TOW
AWAY
ZONE

Grand Central Terminal and the massive bulk of the Pan Am Building these pages sit squarely astride Park Avenue as though signalling its termination. In fact, Park Avenue continues on the far side, on its way towards South Manhattan. Even this solid-seeming stretch of the famous thoroughfare is not quite what it seems, for it really forms a roof over the railway tracks running north from the terminal.

In the late 19th century huge numbers of
southern Italian immigrants crowded into
Lower Manhattan and settled in the district
that came to be known as 'Little Italy'. As in
their homeland, family ties are strong, and in
common with the many ethnic communities
within the city, their customs and traditions are
zealously observed. The festival of San
Gennaro these pages is celebrated every
September, in honor of the patron saint of
Naples. In gratitude for a bountiful harvest, it
is the custom to pin dollar bills to the image of
the saint as it is paraded through the streets.

Each ethnic district retains the flavor and atmosphere brought by the immigrants from their respective countries. In 'Little Italy' these pages traditional shops sell the much-loved pasta and cheeses; friendly bars and open-air restaurants evoke the spirit of Italy and the pungent aroma of Italian cooking spices the air.

From all over the world they came – to start a
new life in a new and vital city – and in they
poured, in their thousands, re-establishing
their cultures and identities in a multitude of
ethnic groups all over New York.

Jews poured into Brooklyn from the Lower
East Side of Manhattan after 1897, when the
Williamsburg Bridge was opened, and arrived
in such numbers that the bridge came to be
known as 'The Jews' Highway'. Though most
have now gone, Hasidic children still play on
the stoops and somber, Hasidic Jews, in their
long black coats and fur hats these pages, can
still be seen on the sidewalks.

It is hard to imagine that the famous Flea Market above, on the Avenue of the Americas, takes place almost in the shadow of the monument to the 20th century, the Empire State Building.

Radio City Music Hall left and below, is situated on the wide, tree-lined Avenue of the Americas right and overleaf, which runs parallel to Fifth Avenue.

84

The entrances to two of America's most famed hotels are featured on this page: above *the Waldorf Astoria* and below, *the Plaza*.

Colorful window displays and a huge, symbolic Christmas tree picked out in lights decorate the main façade of Macy's department store below left during the festive season.

The interior of Scribners, a famous bookshop on Fifth Avenue, is shown above left.

The glossy premises of Elizabeth Arden right, so long a name of international repute, and part of America's multi-million dollar cosmetics industry, grace Fifth Avenue.

The Metropolitan Opera House, shown overleaf by night, is part of the complex of the Lincoln Center for the Performing Arts, which houses, in addition to the Metropolitan Opera, the New York City Opera, the New York Philharmonic Orchestra, the New York City Ballet and a school of music and dance.

Chess and checkers help to while away a sunny afternoon in Harlem above *while shopkeepers dispense their wares* left, below *and* right *in the area's many markets, and shoppers make their way home* above right.

Initiated by the protest artists of the 1930s, mural painting still flourishes, in this case decorating the façade of the Central Harlem Planned Parenthood Center overleaf.

MURAL DESIGN
AND
PROJECT DIRECTOR
NORMAN MESSIAH

ASSISTANT ARTISTS
MR. JAMES BUCKLEY
MR. THIEREY KUHN

UN. 4-3916 Central Harlem 159 W. 127th ST.
PLANNED PARENTHOOD CENTER

First published 1979 by Colour Library International Ltd.
© 1979 Illustrations and text: Colour Library International Ltd., 163 East 64th St., New York, N.Y. 10021.
Colour separations by FERCROM, Barcelona, Spain.
Display and text filmsetting by Focus Photoset, London, England.
Printed and bound by JISA-RIEUSSET, Barcelona, Spain.
All rights reserved.
ISBN 0-8317-6362-0 Library of Congress Catalogue Card No. 79-2146
Published in the United States of America by Mayflower Books, Inc., New York City.